I Do Not Give Up. I Learn From Mistakes!

My Amazing Toddler Behavioral Series

By Suzanne T. Christian

TWO RAVENS BOOKS

Copyright © 2024 by Two Little Ravens, an imprint of Two Ravens Books LLC.

All rights reserved.

No part of this book may be reproduced or used in any way or form or by any means whether electronic or mechanical. This means that you cannot record or photocopy any material ideas or tips that are provided in this book, without the prior written permission of the copyright owner.

Paperback Edition: 9781964202051
Hardcover Edition: 9781964202068
Digital Edition: 9781964202075

Published in the United States by Two Ravens Books LLC, 254 Chapman Rd, Ste 209, Newark DE 19702

'Expand the mind, free the imagination, one title at a time.'
www.tworavensbooks.com

Welcome to
I Do Not Give Up.
I Learn From Mistakes!

This book is a delightful collection of simple affirmations designed specifically for young children. As you explore its pages together, your child will learn the importance of resilience, patience, and the courage to try again.

Each page features vibrant illustrations and relatable scenarios, encouraging a positive attitude toward making mistakes. By making this book a regular part of your reading routine, you empower your toddler to develop a strong foundation of confidence and perseverance, as repetition is a proven teaching tool.

Prepare for a journey of growth, learning, and lots of fun with your toddler!

Suzanne T. Christian

Mistakes are just part of my adventure!

Oops! I can fix that and make it right.

Every time I learn,
I grow big and strong.

When I make mistakes, I find new ways to do it better.

Mistakes are how I learn new things every day.

When my block tower tumbles down, I laugh and build it back up again!

I never give up because I am brave.

When I put my shoe
on the wrong foot,
I giggle and switch
it around!

I keep going, even when it's hard. I do not give up!

Oops! That didn't work, but I can find a new way!

Every mistake helps me grow.

When I try and try, I get better and better!

Oops! I made a mess, but I can clean it up.

I smile when I try again.

I do not give up!
I learn from mistakes
The End!

My Amazing Toddler Behavioral Series

Check Out
Suzanne T. Christian's beloved series
'My Amazing Toddler Behavioral Series'.
Young readers are sure to enjoy!

Two Little Ravens
CHILDREN'S NON-FICTION BOOKS

Dear Amazing Reader,

Thank you for diving into **I Do Not Give Up! I Learn From Mistakes!** with me. If this book touched your heart or made a difference for a young reader, I'd be grateful if you could share your thoughts in a review. Your feedback inspires my future work and helps others discover the magic within these pages.

I'd love to hear from you directly if you have suggestions or ideas for improving the book. Please feel free to reach out to me at **suzanne.christian@tworavensbooks.com.** Your voice counts, and I cherish it deeply.

With heartfelt gratitude,